Christy Hale

water
land

Land and Water Forms
Around the World

A NEAL PORTER BOOK
ROARING BROOK PRESS
NEW YORK

lake

island

isthmus

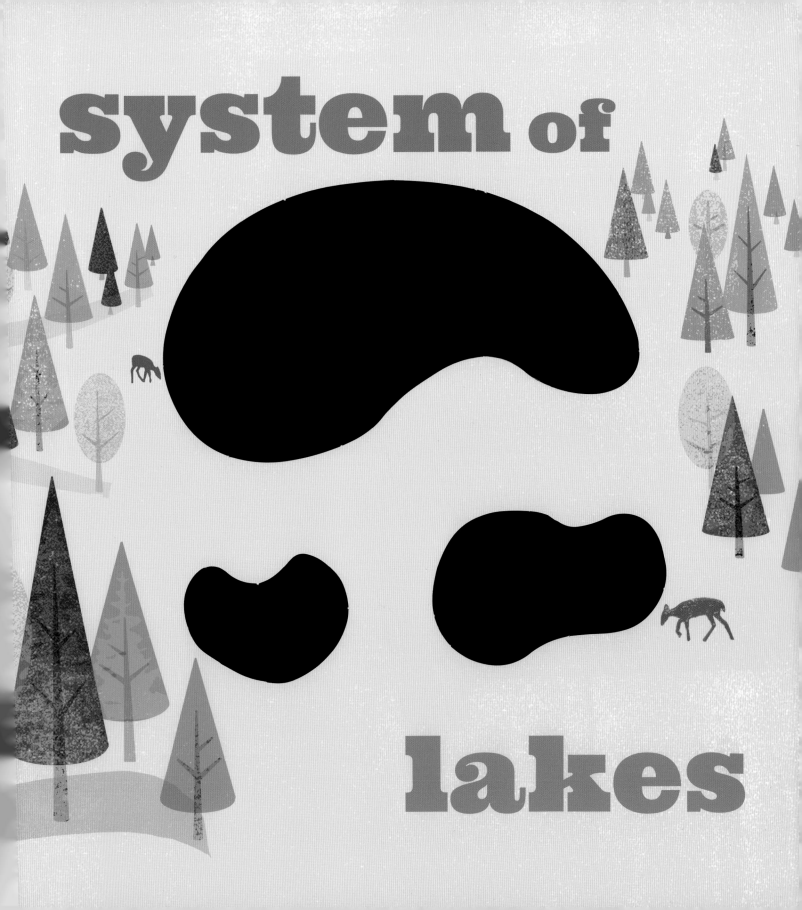

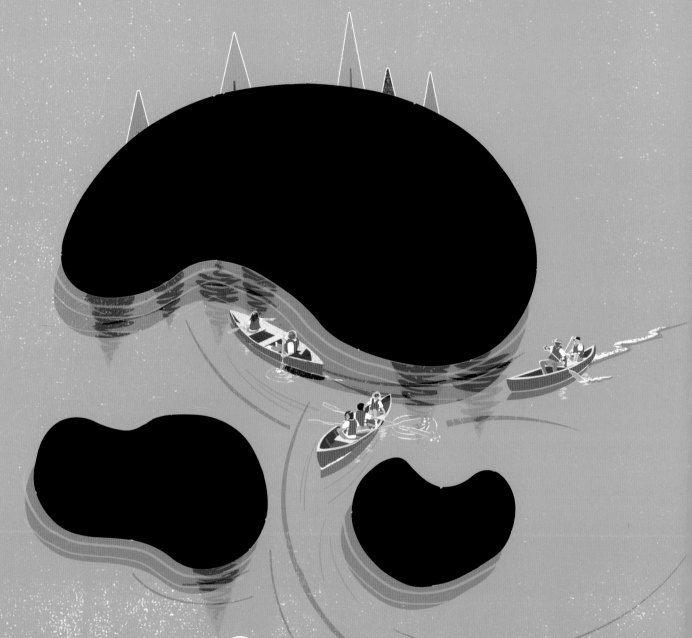

archipelago

A **strait** is a narrow body of water connecting two larger bodies of water.

A **system of lakes** is a group of lakes near one another.

A **gulf** is a body of water almost surrounded by land. It is usually larger than a bay.

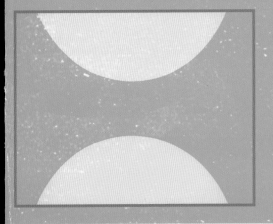

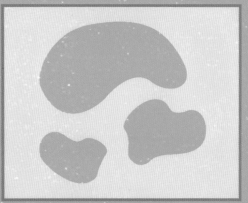

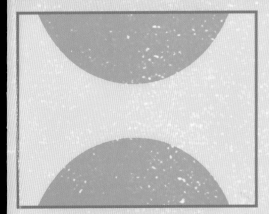

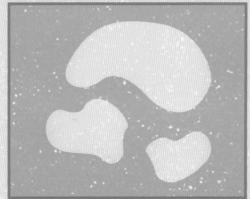

An **isthmus** is a narrow strip of land connecting two larger pieces of land.

An **archipelago** is a group of islands near one another.

A **peninsula** is a piece of land almost surrounded by water. It is usually larger than a cape.

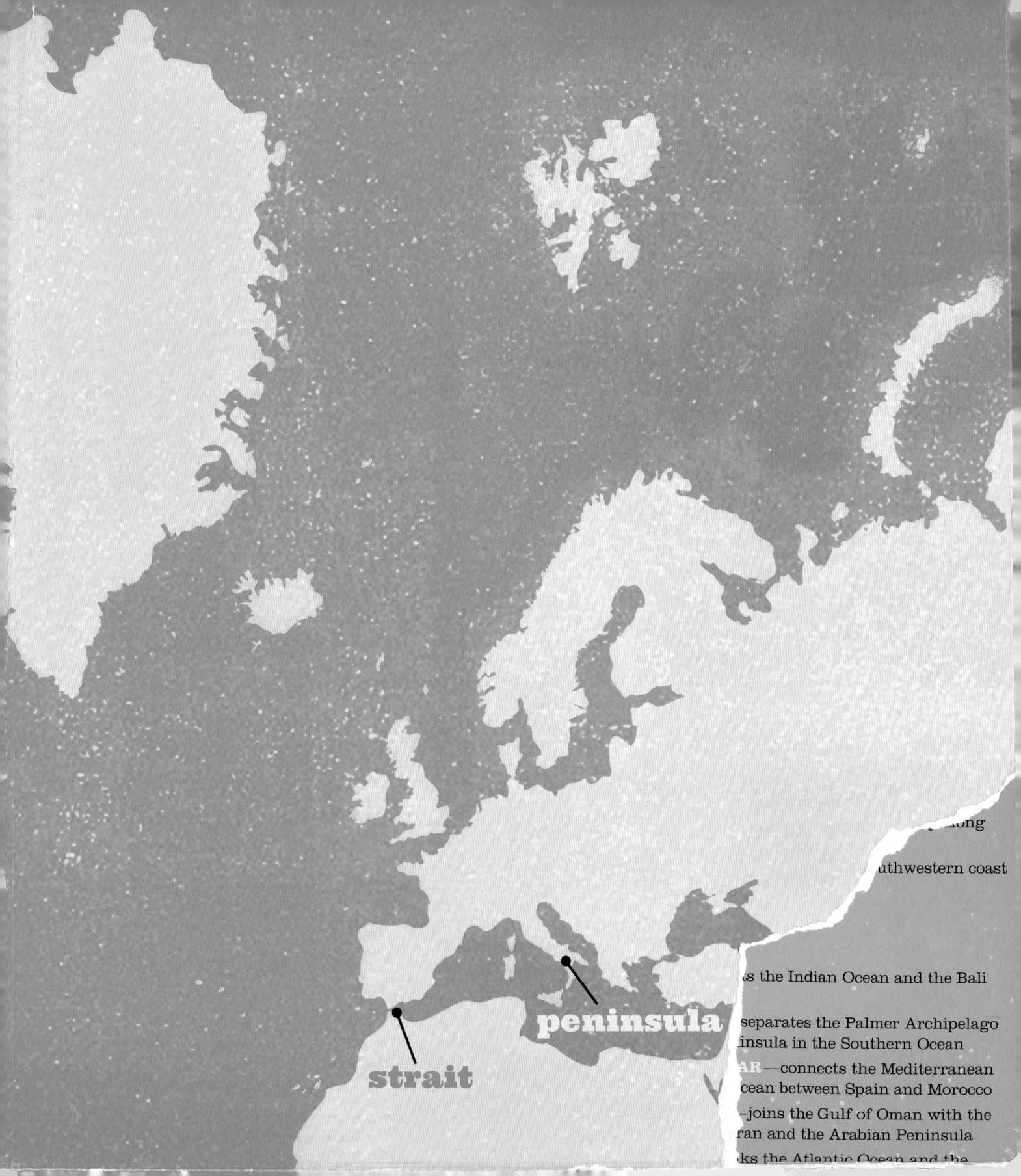

strait

peninsula

...long

...uthwestern coast

...s the Indian Ocean and the Bali

...separates the Palmer Archipelago
...insula in the Southern Ocean

...AR—connects the Mediterranean
...cean between Spain and Morocco

...—joins the Gulf of Oman with the
...ran and the Arabian Peninsula

...ks the Atlantic Ocean and the